Table of Conte

Preface

With more than thirty years of teaching experience, the authors of this handbook have learned that there is considerable confusion with punctuation, business writing, letter formatting, and reference citations. History has proven that there are consistent questions and misunderstandings with regard to these various areas and the use of the English language in general. Consequently, this document has been developed to simplify the writing experience. The handbook is targeted at those individuals who require guidance with style, grammar, usage, and formatting academic and business documents utilizing the Gregg format.

The intent of this handbook is simply to supplement *The Gregg Reference Manual* (10th edition). It is provided as a condensed version of the actual manual. Due to the official manual's length, not all topics are covered. It is not intended to supersede the manual, but rather reduce its length and complexity. This explains the title: *Gregg Reference Manual: The Easy Way!*

The handbook is divided into six sections. Section one focuses on the mechanics of Gregg format; section two reviews major punctuation marks; section three is geared toward the proper development of letters, memos, and email documents; section four targets reports and manuscripts; section five highlights notes and bibliographies; and, lastly, section six reviews tables.

Note: Several names given throughout the document are fictitious.

Gregg Reference Manual: The Easy Way!

Peggy M. Houghton, Ph.D.
Timothy J. Houghton, Ph.D.

Editor: Michele M. Pratt

Education is one of the best investments you will ever make…and our books maximize that investment!

Houghton & Houghton

Baker College
Flint, MI

© Copyright 2009
Peggy M. Houghton, Ph.D.

ISBN: 978-0-923568-93-1

www.houghtonandhoughton.com

For more information, contact:
Baker College Bookstore
bookstore@baker.edu
800-339-9879
Volume discounts are available through Baker College

LIBRARY OF CONGRESS CATALOGING-IN-PUBLICATION DATA

Houghton, Peggy M.
    Gregg reference manual : the easy way! / Peggy M. Houghton, Timothy J. Houghton.
        p. cm.
    Includes bibliographical references and index.
    ISBN 978-0-923568-93-1
    1. Sabin, William A. Gregg reference manual—Handbooks, manuals, etc. 2. English language—Business English—Handbooks, manuals, etc. 3. English language—Grammar—Handbooks, manuals, etc. 4. English language—Transcription—Handbooks, manuals, etc. 5. Business writing—Handbooks, manuals, etc. I. Houghton, Timothy J., 1961- II. Sabin, William A. Gregg reference manual. III. Title.

PE1479.B87S2334 2009
808'.042--dc22
                                    2009011700

Manufactured in the United States of America

Section One
Mechanics

Utilizing Microsoft Word (for applications prior to Microsoft Word 2007)

While all documents utilizing Gregg may vary with regard to margins, 1-inch margins are commonly utilized. The following section provides specific instructions on how to set up a document using 1-inch margins in Microsoft Word.

Margins

All margins (top, bottom, and sides) should be set to at least 1 inch. Microsoft Word allows the user to set the margin at a default of 1 inch. To do so, follow the guidelines below:

1. Under FILE, select PAGE SETUP.

2. Select MARGINS tab and type 1" at TOP, BOTTOM, LEFT, and RIGHT boxes. Click OK.

Margins

Utilizing Microsoft Word 2007

Below are specific instructions on how to set 1-inch margins using Microsoft Word 2007.

Margins

1. Select PAGE LAYOUT from the ribbon tabs.

2. Select the MARGINS icon from the PAGE SETUP drop-down menu.

3. Select CUSTOM MARGINS. Type 1" for the TOP, RIGHT, LEFT, and BOTTOM margins. Before leaving this setup, select APPLY TO: Whole Document, then click OK.

Section Two: Major Punctuation Marks and Style

Period

A period (.) should be used in the following instances:

- following a statement or command
- following a polite request or command
- at the end of an indirect question
- with decimals

Periods

Question Mark

A question mark (?) should be used in the following instances:

- to indicate direct questions
- to indicate questions within sentences
- to express doubt

Question Marks

Exclamation Point

An exclamation point (!) should be used in the following instance:

- to express strong feeling

Exclamation Points

Comma

A comma (,) should be used in the following instances:

- to set off nonessential expressions: those words not necessary to convey the meaning of the sentence
- to set off words, phrases, or clauses when they interrupt the flow of a sentence
- to set off words, phrases, or clauses that dangle at the end of a sentence
- to set off transitional expressions

Commas

Commas

- to set off descriptive expressions that follow the words they refer to and provide nonessential information
- to separate words, phrases, or clauses within a sentence
- to separate two independent clauses that are connected by a conjunction
- to separate a dependent clause that precedes an independent clause
- if the dependent clause is nonessential and either follows the main clause or is placed within the main clause
- if words and phrases at the beginning, at the end, or within the sentence are nonessential
- in dates when the year follows the month and day [two commas set off the year]

> I plan to graduate January 20, 2010, from the University of Michigan.

- in a series

Semicolon

A semicolon (;) should be used in the following instances:

Semicolons

- between two independent clauses when no conjunction is utilized
- with independent clauses linked by transitional expressions
- in a series of items that already contain a comma(s)

Colon

A colon (:) should be used in the following instances:

Colons

- between independent clauses when the second clause clarifies the first clause and no conjunction or transitional expression is utilized to link the clauses
- prior to lists and enumerations
- in expressions of proportions and time

- in business documents
- in reference to books or publications

Dash

A dash (–) should be used in the following instances:

- in place of a comma to show strong emphasis on nonessential elements of the sentence
- in place of a semicolon to show a stronger break between clauses
- in place of a colon to introduce words, phrases, or clauses
- in place of parentheses to give nonessential elements strong emphasis
- to indicate an abrupt break or an afterthought
- to indicate hesitation
- to emphasize a specific word(s)
- with repetitions, restatements, and summarizing words

Dashes

Notes regarding dashes:

Never use a comma, semicolon, or colon before an opening dash. Additionally, do not use a period before an opening dash unless the period follows an abbreviation.

Unless a period follows an abbreviation, do not use a period before the closing dash when writing a statement or a command that is set off by dashes within a sentence.

Use a question mark or exclamation point before the closing dash when a question or an exclamation is set off by dashes within a sentence.

Retain the closing dash and omit the comma when a closing dash occurs at a point where the sentence requires a comma.

Drop the closing dash and use the appropriate sentence punctuation if a closing dash occurs at a point where the sentence requires a semicolon, colon, or closing parenthesis.

Dashes

Use an *em dash* (a dash as wide as a capital *M*) when typing dashes. The *em dash* is typically included in most software packages. However, if it is not, a dash is constructed by striking the hyphen key *twice* with no spaces between the hyphens. Never use a single hyphen as a dash.

A *two-em dash* (a dash as wide as two capital *M*s) indicates that letters are missing from a word; if an *em dash* is unavailable, use four consecutive hyphens (with no spacing between hyphens). If letters are missing at the end of the word, leave a space after the last dash.

A *three-em dash* (a dash as wide as three capital *M*s) indicates that a complete word has been left out or needs to be provided; if an *em dash* is unavailable, use six consecutive hyphens (with no spacing between hyphens). Leave one space before the first dash and one space after the last dash, since it represents a missing word.

An *en dash* (half the length of an *em dash* but longer than a hyphen) is used to connect a range of numbers. The *en dash* signifies "up to and including" in various expressions.

Parentheses

Parentheses ( ) should be used in the following instances:

Parentheses

- with explanatory material
- with reference information and directions
- with dates
- with enumerated items

Notes regarding parentheses:

Punctuation that follows a parenthesis (i.e. comma, semicolon, etc.) should be placed *outside* the closing parenthesis.

Unless using an abbreviation, do not use a period before the closing parenthesis.

Only use a question mark or exclamation point before the closing parenthesis if the mark applies specifically to the word(s) enclosed in parentheses *and* the sentence ends with a different mark of punctuation. Otherwise, the punctuation mark should be placed after the closing parenthesis.

If the words in parentheses are to be treated as a *separate sentence,* the preceding sentence should close with the appropriate punctuation mark. The words in parentheses should begin with a capital letter. Punctuation for the sentence enclosed within parentheses should be placed before the closing parenthesis, and no additional punctuation should follow the closing parenthesis.

Quotation Marks

Quotation marks (" ") should be used in the following instances:

- to enclose a direct quotation; direct quotation means exact words of another individual

- with titles of literary and artistic works

- to emphasize words and phrases

Notes regarding quotation marks:

Periods and commas are always placed inside the quotation marks.

When using terms not familiar with the reader, enclose them in quotation marks the first time they are used.

Slang expressions and the use of deliberate improper grammar and spelling are enclosed in quotation marks so that the reader understands the writer intentionally made the error(s).

Quotation marks are placed around the titles that represent only *part* of a complete published work (such as article, song, or chapter titles). Titles of *complete published* works (such as books or journals) are italicized. However, quotation marks are placed around the titles of *complete but unpublished* works.

Use quotation marks around the titles of songs and short musical compositions. Additionally, use quotation marks around the titles of individual segments or programs that are part of a TV or radio series.

A quotation within a quotation is enclosed in a pair of single quotation marks.

Semicolons and colons are always placed outside the closing quotation mark.

At the end of a sentence, a question mark or exclamation point is placed *inside* the closing quotation mark when it applies only to the quoted material; at the end of a sentence, a question mark or exclamation point is placed *outside* the closing quotation mark if it applies to the entire sentence.

When a quoted sentence is independent (stands alone), the appropriate punctuation is placed *inside* the closing quotation mark.

Quotation Marks

Omit the period before the closing quotation mark and use a comma instead if the quoted statement occurs at the beginning of a sentence. A comma generally precedes the opening quotation mark when a quoted statement, question, or exclamation is located at the end of a sentence and introduced by an expression such as *he said*.

Commas are not required to set off a quotation that occurs within a sentence if the quotation is an essential expression. However, if the quotation is *not* essential to the meaning of the sentence, then it should be set off with commas.

The preferred way to handle a long quotation (four lines or longer) is to indent it a half inch from each side margin. The actual quotation should be single-spaced. Do not enclose it in quotation marks; the indentation implies that it is a direct quotation. A blank line should be left above and below the quotation.

Use ellipses marks if multiple words are omitted within a quotation. An ellipsis is typed as three periods with one space before and after each period.

Italics and Underlining

Italics or underlining should be used in the following instances:

- for special emphasis

- with titles of literary and artistic works

- with foreign expressions

Use italics as the preferred style due to the availability in word processing software.

Numbers

Figure Style for Numbers

- This style is commonly used in ordinary business correspondence.

- Spell out numbers from one through ten; use figures for numbers 11 and higher.

- When numbers have technical significance (i.e. dates, proportions, money, etc.), use all figures (even for the numbers 1–10).

- At the beginning of a sentence, use words for numbers, fractions, nontechnical references to age, periods of time, measurements, and most ordinals.

- Use the same format to express related numbers, whether or not they are above or below 10. If any of the numbers are above 10, use all figures when completing the sentence.

Word Style for Numbers

- This style is typically used with high-level executive correspondence.

- Spell out numbers from 1 through 100; use figures for numbers higher than 100.

- Whether exact or approximate, spell out numbers that can be expressed in one or two words.

ninety-nine people

- Express related numbers in the same way (even if some numbers are over 100, and other numbers are below). If any of the numbers should be typed in figure format, use all figures for consistency purposes.

> My grocery list included 6 bananas, 8 pears, and 12 apples.

Special Rules for Numbers

- When a day stands alone or precedes a month, it should be expressed either in ordinal figures (1st, 2nd, etc.) or in ordinal words (the first, the second, etc.).

- When the day follows a month, a cardinal figure (1, 2, etc.) should be used to express it.

- Express complete dates in the month-day-year order.

Numbers

> April 30, 2010

- The U.S. military utilizes the day-month-year sequence.

> 30 April 2010

- When citing a month, day, and year within a sentence, two commas set off the year.

> A letter dated May 23, 1965, was found underneath the bed.

- Years in history that are well recognized can be abbreviated.

> the stock market crash in '29

Money and Numbers

- Figures are used to express exact or approximate amounts of money.

> $10

- Indefinite amounts of money should be spelled out.

**Numbers:
Money**

> several hundred dollars

- Decimal points and/or zeros are not required if it is a whole dollar amount.

> This bike costs $125.

- With amounts under one dollar, use figures and the word *cents*.

> 75 cents per pound

Beginning of Sentences and Numbers

- Spell out numbers that begin a sentence.

> Eight hundred faculty members attended the conference.

Numbers

Fractions

- Spell out fractions that stand alone.

> one-tenth

- When a fraction is spelled out, hyphenate the numerator and the denominator. However, if either the numerator or denominator contains a hyphen, do not hyphenate the words.

> six-sevenths   twelve twenty-seconds

Numbers: Fractions

- Use figures to express a mixed number. However, if the number begins a sentence, spell out the mixed number.

> 2¼
>
> Ten and one-half inches of snow fell at the Denver airport.

Measurements and Expressions of Age and Time

- When measurements and expressions of age and time have technical or statistical significance, they are expressed in figures.

> It was a 180-degree change from his initial decision.

Numbers: Measurements

- When measurements and expressions of age and time do not have technical or statistical significance, they are expressed in words.

> He performed to the tenth degree on this assignment.

Clock Time

- Always use figures with *a.m.* or *p.m.*

**Numbers:
Clock Time**

| 10:15 a.m. | 6 p.m. |

- When using *o'clock*, use figures to convey emphasis or words to convey formality.

| 7 o'clock–used for emphasis |
| seven o'clock–used for formality |

- Spell out the time or convert the time to all figures when expressing time without using *a.m.* or *p.m.*

| a quarter past six | 6:15 |

Decimals

- Write decimals in figures; never use commas in the decimal part of a number.

**Numbers:
Decimals**

| 239.45890 | 12,569.00165 |

- When no whole number precedes a decimal point and the decimal stands alone, insert a zero before the decimal point.

| 0.6 grams |

Percentages

- Spell out the word *percent* and express percentages in figures.

**Numbers:
Percentages**

| The jacket also includes a 25 percent discount. |

- Use the % symbol with tables, with business forms, and with statistical or technical material.

- Spell out the number when the percentage does not represent a technical measurement.

| I concur one hundred percent with your comments. |

Abbreviations
Basic Rules

- Do not abbreviate a term in some instances and not others–be consistent.

- If the reading audience is unfamiliar with the abbreviation, spell out the full term along with the abbreviation when it is first utilized.

Abbreviations:
Basic Rules

- When a word or phrase is condensed by the use of a contraction, an apostrophe is placed where letters are omitted. No period follows the contraction except at the end of a sentence.

- Contractions are generally only used in informal writing or in tables when space is limited.

Punctuation and Spacing with Abbreviations

- Abbreviate a single word with a period at the end.

> Dr.

- Lowercase abbreviations that are made up of single initials require a period after each initial. However, no space is required after each internal period.

> p.m.

Abbreviations:
Punctuation and
Spacing

- Abbreviations that are comprised of all capital letters and single initials require no periods and no internal spaces.

> ILA–International Leadership Association

- One space should follow an abbreviation within a sentence unless another mark of punctuation follows immediately.

- No space should follow an abbreviation at the end of a question or an exclamation. Insert a question mark or exclamation point directly after the abbreviation.

Personal Names and Initials

- Initials in a person's name should be followed by a period and one space.

> Larry M. Kaye

Abbreviations:
Personal Names

- Use the title *Ms.* when it is preferred by a woman, when the marital status of a woman is not known, or when the woman's marital status is irrelevant to the context of the sentence.

- *Jr., Sr.,* and *Esq.* should always be abbreviated when they follow personal names.

> Michael S. Stemmer, Sr.

Academic Degrees

- A period is required after each element in academic degrees and religious orders; however, there is no spacing between elements.

> M.D.

- If an academic degree follows a person's name, do not use titles such as *Dr., Mr., Ms.,* etc.

Abbreviations:
Academic Degrees

> Dr. Helen Bojarczyk *or* Helen Borjarczyk, Ph.D.

- If multiple academic degrees follow a person's name, list the degrees in order in which they were granted.

> James L. Schiro, B.S., M.B.A, J.D.

- Use academic degrees only when the person's full name is listed.

> Peter W. Karsten, C.P.A.

Names of Organizations

- Names of organizations that are well-known may be abbreviated (if not used in formal writing). The abbreviations should be typed in uppercase letters with no periods or spaces.

Abbreviations: Names of Organizations

> YMCA–Young Men's Christian Association

- Several organizations that have long been referred to in their abbreviated form have now adopted their respective abbreviations as their formal name.

> ABC–American Broadcasting Company

Acronyms

- Acronyms can be used in all writing.

- If the reading audience is unfamiliar with the acronym, list the full expression when the acronym is first utilized. Subsequently, the acronym alone is sufficient.

Abbreviations: Acronyms

> Mothers Against Drunk Driving (MADD) is a worthy organization.

Geographical Names

- When state names are abbreviated in addresses, use the United States Postal Service two-letter abbreviation.

> Michigan–MI

Abbreviations: Geographical Names

- Other geographic abbreviations designated with single initials require a period after each initial. However, there is no space after each internal period.

> N.A.–North America

- When geographic abbreviations require more than one initial, space once after each internal period.

> S. Dak.

- Other than in tables (where space is limited), do not abbreviate place names such as *Fort, Mount, Point,* or *Port.*

> Port Crescent

Time and Time Zones

Abbreviations:
Time and Time
Zones

- The standard continental United States time zones are designated as *EST, CST, MST,* and *PST.*

- Use *DST* (daylight saving time) when daylight saving time is in effect.

Customary Measurements

- When units of measure occur frequently throughout a document (such as in technical and scientific writing), the abbreviated form is acceptable without periods.

Abbreviations:
Customary
Measurements

> ft – foot/feet

- Spell out units of measure in writings that are not technical in nature.

Section Three:
Letters, Memos, and Email

Business Letters

Business letters generally contain four standard sections and numerous optional features. Standard sections include the heading, opening, body, and closing. Optional features include a personal or confidential notation, reference notation, attention line, subject line, company signature, file name notation, enclosure notation, delivery notation, confirmation notation, copy notation, and postscript.

The actual letter is typically designed in one of four ways:

- *Modified-Block Style with no indents*: The date line, complimentary closing, company signature, and writer identification all begin at the center of the document. Everything else begins flush left.

- *Modified-Block Style with indents* (also referred to as *semiblock style*): This style is the same as *modified-block style* with one exception: the first line of each paragraph is indented 0.5 inch.

- *Block Style* (also referred to as *full-block style*): Generally all lines begin at the left margin. Other than displayed quotations, tables, and similar matter, nothing is indented.

- *Simplified Style*: This style is similar to *block style* with three exceptions: a subject line (in all uppercase letters) replaces the salutation, the complimentary closing is deleted, and the writer's signature block is typed (in all uppercase letters) on one line.

Note: Most word processing software packages provide easy-to-use templates of various types of letter style formats. These templates allow the writer to simply fill in the desired text of each component of the letter. The authors of this handbook strongly encourage writers to utilize these templates, as they result in far less time with developing an original document.

Letterhead of Company

FIRST SOUTHERN
BANK OF ORLANDO

156 Park St.
Sarasota, FL 32765

Date Line: Date letter is typed. Should start four lines from the letterhead and begin in the center. After the date line, return four times.

March 12, 2009

Inside Address: Name and address of letter recipient. After the address, return twice.

Ms. Marsha Moore
DPM Advertising Agency
1568 South Lake Blvd.
Orlando, FL 32386

Salutation: Greeting. After the salutation, return twice.

Ms. Marsha Moore:

In order to include your advertising brochure in our March statements, I will need a signed letter from you stating the quantity desired as well as a copy of the proposed brochure.

Body: Text of the letter. Single-space *within* each paragraph. Return twice *after* each paragraph. Do not indent paragraphs.

Per our earlier telephone conversation, the brochures will be included in both the March and April statements. Would you like the brochures to go to all branches or just a selection of specific branches?

I am sending a copy of this letter to Ed Mahalic, our operations manager, so that he can advise me regarding the necessary steps for approval of your request. If approval is granted, we have an approximate total (all branches) of 3,500 checking accounts and 2,000 savings accounts.

Reference Initials: Initials of the person who typed the letter (if other than the signer). After the reference initials, return twice.

Please send me a copy of the proposed brochure, as well as the information requested above, by April 1, 2009, so that we can satisfy your request.

Sincerely,

Complimentary Closing: Parting farewell. Begin typing at the center of the page. After the complimentary closing, return four times. This allows space for a signature.

Clara Albertson
Vice President

mgh

Notation: Signifies that a copy of the letter is being sent to another person.

c Ed Mahalic

Writer's Identification: Name and/or title of the writer. Begin typing at the center of the page. After the writer's identification, return twice.

Modified-Block Style (no indents)

Letterhead of Company

March 12, 2009

Date Line: Date letter is typed. Should start four lines from the letterhead and begin in the center. After the date line, return four times.

Ms. Marsha Moore
DPM Advertising Agency
1568 South Lake Blvd.
Orlando, FL 32386

Inside Address: Name and address of letter recipient. After the address, return twice.

Ms. Marsha Moore:

Salutation: Greeting. After the salutation, return twice.

In order to include your advertising brochure in our March statements, I will need a signed letter from you stating the quantity desired as well as a copy of the proposed brochure.

Per our earlier telephone conversation, the brochures will be included in both the March and April statements. Would you like the brochures to go to all branches or just a selection of specific branches?

I am sending a copy of this letter to Ed Mahalic, our operations manager, so that he can advise me regarding the necessary steps for approval of your request. If approval is granted, we have an approximate total (all branches) of 3,500 checking accounts and 2,000 savings accounts.

Please send me a copy of the proposed brochure, as well as the information requested above, by April 1, 2009, so that we can satisfy your request.

Body: Text of the letter. Indent the first line of each paragraph. Single-space *within* each paragraph. Return twice *after* each paragraph.

Sincerely,

Complimentary Closing: Parting farewell. Begin typing at the center of the page. After the complimentary closing, return four times. This allows space for a signature.

Clara Albertson
Vice President

Reference Initials: Initials of the person who typed the letter (if other than the signer). After the reference initials, return twice.

mgh

c Ed Mahalic

Writer's Identification: Name and/or title of the writer. Begin typing at the center of the page. After the writer's identification, return twice.

Notation: Signifies that a copy of the letter is being sent to another person.

Modified-Block Style (with indents)

RST SOUTHERN
ANK OF ORLANDO

156 Park St.
Sarasota, FL 32765

Date Line: Date letter is typed. Should start four lines from the letterhead. After the date line, return four times.

March 12, 2009

Inside Address: Name and address of letter recipient. After the address, return twice.

Ms. Marsha Moore
DPM Advertising Agency
1568 South Lake Blvd.
Orlando, FL 32386

Salutation: Greeting. After the salutation, return twice.

Ms. Marsha Moore:

In order to include your advertising brochure in our March statements, I will need a signed letter from you stating the quantity desired as well as a copy of the proposed brochure.

Body: Text of the letter. Single-space *within* each paragraph. Return twice *after* each paragraph.

Per our earlier telephone conversation, the brochures will be included in both the March and April statements. Would you like the brochures to go to all branches or just a selection of specific branches?

I am sending a copy of this letter to Ed Mahalic, our operations manager, so that he can advise me regarding the necessary steps for approval of your request. If approval is granted, we have an approximate total (all branches) of 3,500 checking accounts and 2,000 savings accounts.

Complimentary Closing: Parting farewell. After the complimentary closing, return four times. This allows space for a signature.

Please send me a copy of the proposed brochure, as well as the information requested above, by April 1, 2009, so that we can satisfy your request.

Sincerely,

Clara Albertson
Vice President

Writer's Identification: Name and/or title of the writer. After the writer's identification, return twice.

Reference Initials: Initials of the person who typed the letter (if other than the signer). After the reference initials, return twice.

mgh

c Ed Mahalic

Notation: Signifies that a copy of the letter is being sent to another person.

Block Style

Letterhead of Company

March 12, 2009

Date Line: Date letter is typed. Should start four lines from the letterhead. After the date line, return six times.

Ms. Marsha Moore
DPM Advertising Agency
1568 South Lake Blvd.
Orlando, FL 32386

Inside Address: Name and address of letter recipient. After the address, return three times.

SUBJECT: ADVERTISING BROCHURES

Subject Line: A subject line (in all caps) replaces the salutation. After the subject line, return three times.

In order to include your advertising brochure in our March statements, I will need a signed letter from you stating the quantity desired as well as a copy of the proposed brochure.

Per our earlier telephone conversation, the brochures will be included in both the March and April statements. Would you like the brochures to go to all branches or just a selection of specific branches?

Body: Text of the letter. Single-space *within* each paragraph. Return twice *after* each paragraph.

I am sending a copy of this letter to Ed Mahalic, our operations manager, so that he can advise me regarding the necessary steps for approval of your request. If approval is granted, we have an approximate total (all branches) of 3,500 checking accounts and 2,000 savings accounts.

Please send me a copy of the proposed brochure, as well as the information requested above, by April 1, 2009, so that we can satisfy your request.

After the last paragraph, return five times. This allows space for a signature.

CLARA ALBERTSON, VICE PRESIDENT

mgh

c Ed Mahalic

Writer's Identification: Name and/or title of the writer. Typed in all caps and placed on one line. After the identification line, return twice.

Reference Initials: Initials of the person who typed the letter (if other than the signer). After the reference initials, return twice.

Notation: Signifies that a copy of the letter is being sent to another person.

Simplified Style

Memos

Printed memos were originally used for communication exchanges within an organization. Due to advanced technology, the printed memo is essentially a thing of the past. However, its format is utilized in documents that are transmitted via email.

The memo format and the email format (discussed in the next section) are very similar. The heading in each type of correspondence contains the same type of information: name of the recipient(s), subject of the message, and date of the transmittal.

Email messages are typically used when the message is not of great importance and will ultimately be deleted. One such example would be the meeting date of an upcoming seminar. Memos are typically used when the content of the message is important and may be necessary for future retrieval. A company policy change would be an example where a memo style format is more appropriate.

Many organizations develop their own memo format; others use standard memo designs. A sample memo is provided below. Just as with letters, however, most word processing software packages provide sample memo templates.

Note: Again, the authors of this handbook urge writers to utilize the provided templates, as they save time by avoiding the necessity of designing an original document.

FIRST SOUTHERN
BANK OF ORLANDO

156 Park St.
Sarasota, FL 32765

Letterhead of Company

To: Ms. Marsha Moore

Recipient of Memo: Should start four lines from the letterhead. After typing the name of the recipient, return twice.

From: Ms. Clara Albertson

Person Writing the Memo: After typing the name of the person writing the memo, return twice.

Cc: Mr. Ed Mahalic

Carbon Copy Notation: Signifies that a copy of the memo is being sent to another person. After typing the notation, return twice.

Date: March 12, 2009

Re: Advertising Brochures

In order to include your advertising brochure in our March statements, I will need a signed letter from you stating the quantity desired as well as a copy of the proposed brochure.

Date Line: Date letter is typed. After the date line, return twice.

Per our earlier telephone conversation, the brochures will be included in both the March and April statements. Would you like the brochures to go to all branches or just a selection of specific branches?

Regarding Line: Indicates the memo subject matter. After the regarding line, return three times.

I am sending a copy of this letter to Ed Mahalic, our operations manager, so that he can advise me regarding the necessary steps for approval of your request. If approval is granted, we have an approximate total (all branches) of 3,500 checking accounts and 2,000 savings accounts.

Please send me a copy of the proposed brochure, as well as the information requested above, by April 1, 2009, so that we can satisfy your request.

Body: Text of the memo. Single-space *within* each paragraph. Return twice *after* each paragraph.

mgh

Reference Initials: Initials of the person who typed the letter (if other than the person who wrote the memo).

Memo

Email

Email involves electronic communication. It is used as an alternative to other traditional forms of communication, such as *snail mail* and faxes. Due to advances in technology, the use of email has grown exponentially over the past decade. It eliminates costly mailing expenses and does away with what is commonly known as *phone tag*. In short, email is today's preferred mode of transmission.

Email

Some people consider email to be an informal form of communication. As such, they have a tendency to not abide by standard guidelines for the English language. Far less proofreading occurs with email correspondence. Hence, many times these messages are hastily written and numerous punctuation and grammatical errors are strewn throughout the document. This *let it go as is* policy may be acceptable for personal communication but should be avoided with business correspondence. In other words, personal email writing can be casual. However, when writing an email on behalf of a business organization, the writer must adhere strictly to all writing standards that apply to other forms of business communication.

Writers must also be aware of *email netiquette*. Email netiquette simply means realizing that email communication is with real people, albeit through a faceless medium. While emotions may come into play when sending and receiving emails, people must always respect the rights of others. All writing should be clear, concise, and courteous. Email correspondence can be easily forwarded and archived for future retrieval purposes. Thus, the writer should clearly appreciate the feelings of all recipients of the communication.

Email addresses consist of several elements.

1. The address begins with a *user name*. The user name is a distinct name that is used to sign on to an email system.

2. The symbol for *at* (@) follows the user name.

3. The ending portion of an email address consists of two parts. The first part is the name of the host computer, followed by a period and a top level domain (the type of organization that owns the host computer). The top level domain is printed in abbreviated form. Common abbreviated forms include *.com* (commercial enterprise), *.org* (a nonprofit organization), and *.edu* (educational institution).

The following are examples of email addresses:

> john.henderson@gmail.com
>
> jreynolds@wish.org
>
> henderson12@northwood.edu

Email

Notes regarding email:

Never alter the spacing or punctuation in an email address.

Do not type a message in all capital letters. This implies that the writer is writing with emotion, and the message may be misunderstood.

Carbon copy is notated as *cc*. This implies that a copy of the message is also being sent to the recipient who follows the cc notation.

Blind carbon copy is notated as *bcc*. This implies that a copy of the message is also being *privately* sent to the recipient who follows the *bcc* notation. The primary recipient of the message will not know that a blind carbon copy has been sent.

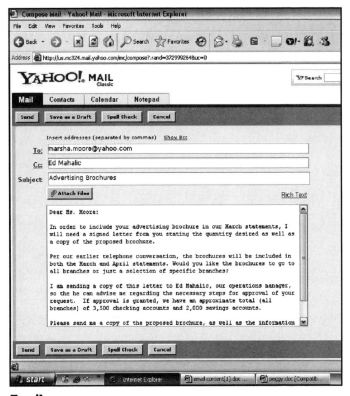

Email

Section Four:
Reports and Manuscripts

Formal Reports

In General
Contents

- *Front Matter*–title page, letter or memo of transmittal, table of contents, list of tables and illustrations, foreword, preface, and summary

- *Body*–introduction, main discussion, and conclusion

- *Back Matter*–appendices, endnotes, bibliography, and glossary

Side Margins

- Unbound Reports–1 inch or 1.25 inches (default) for both sides. Use left justification only (no right or full).

- Bound Reports–1.5 inch for left side, 1 inch or 1.25 inch (default) for right side. Use left justification only (no right or full).

Top and Bottom Margins (opening page only)

- Applies to the first page of chapters and the first page of each part of front and back matter.

- Top margin is 2 inches. Nothing is typed in the top margin.

- Use the page numbering feature of a word processing program and click on the format that ends an opening page with a centered page number at the bottom.

Top and Bottom Margins (other pages)

- Top and bottom margins are 1 inch.

- *Body* and *back matter* sections use the page numbering feature of a word processing program to place the page number in the upper right corner of the page. Use the *header* feature to add additional information.

- *Front matter* sections use the page numbering feature of a word processing program to center the page number at the bottom of the page. Use the *footer* feature to add additional information.

Front Matter

Title Pages

- Business Reports–list title, subtitle (if applicable), author, author's title, author's department, and submission date.

- Academic Reports–list title, subtitle (if applicable), author, instructor, course, and submission date.

- Titles are centered in bold uppercase letters (single space if more than one line).

- Subtitles are centered in bold uppercase and lowercase letters (single space if more than one line). Doublespace between titles and subtitles.

- Author identification (name, title, and department or division) is centered in bold uppercase and lowercase letters. Doublespace between *Submitted by* and the author's name.

- Reader identification (name, title, and department or division) is centered in bold uppercase and lowercase letters. Doublespace between *Prepared for* and the reader's name.

- List the submission date (month, day, and year) below the reader identification in bold uppercase and lowercase letters. Doublespace between the reader identification and the date.

- Top and bottom margins are at least 1 inch and equal to or larger than the space inserted between the blocks of text.

- Graphic elements, such as logos, may be used to enhance the appearance of a business report title page.

- Two block arrangement–use two blocks of type with 1 to 2 inches between blocks. Center all text vertically and horizontally.

- Three block arrangement–use three blocks of type with equal space above and below the middle block. Center all text vertically and horizontally.

- The following page is an example of a three-block business report.

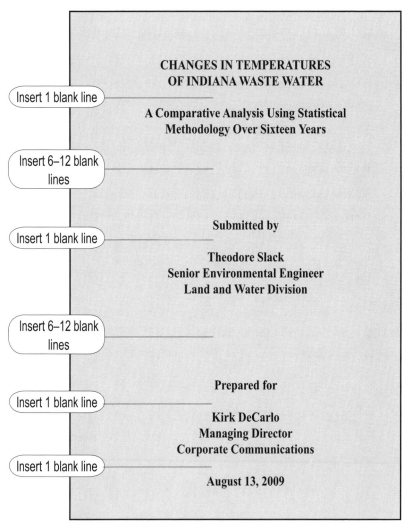

**CHANGES IN TEMPERATURES
OF INDIANA WASTE WATER**

Insert 1 blank line

**A Comparative Analysis Using Statistical
Methodology Over Sixteen Years**

Insert 6–12 blank
lines

Submitted by

Insert 1 blank line

**Theodore Slack
Senior Environmental Engineer
Land and Water Division**

Insert 6–12 blank
lines

Prepared for

Insert 1 blank line

**Kirk DeCarlo
Managing Director
Corporate Communications**

Insert 1 blank line

August 13, 2009

Three-Block Business Report

- The following is an example of a three-block academic report:

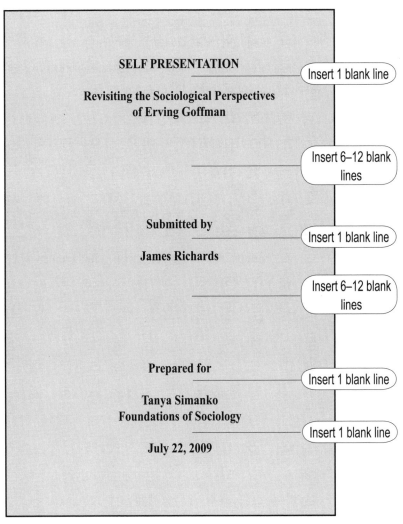

SELF PRESENTATION

Insert 1 blank line

Revisiting the Sociological Perspectives of Erving Goffman

Insert 6–12 blank lines

Submitted by

Insert 1 blank line

James Richards

Insert 6–12 blank lines

Prepared for

Insert 1 blank line

Tanya Simanko
Foundations of Sociology

Insert 1 blank line

July 22, 2009

Three-Block Academic Report

Letters or Memos of Transmittal

- Typically accompanies the formal report. Clip it to the front of the report, insert it in the binder preceding the title page, or email it as a message or attachment.

- Use a memo format if the report is only being distributed internally. Do not indent text paragraphs.

- Use a letter format (on company letterhead) if the report is being sent outside of the organization.

- The memo or letter format must:

  1. Briefly describe the report sent or distributed.

  2. Briefly reference the circumstances surrounding the report.

  3. Briefly explain why the report is being sent to the addressee.

  4. Briefly state the action expected to be taken by the addressee.

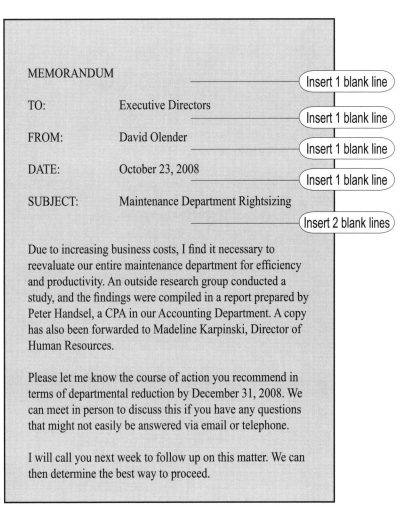

MEMORANDUM   _____ Insert 1 blank line

TO: Executive Directors   _____ Insert 1 blank line

FROM: David Olender   _____ Insert 1 blank line

DATE: October 23, 2008   _____ Insert 1 blank line

SUBJECT: Maintenance Department Rightsizing
                                              _____ Insert 2 blank lines

Due to increasing business costs, I find it necessary to
reevaluate our entire maintenance department for efficiency
and productivity. An outside research group conducted a
study, and the findings were compiled in a report prepared by
Peter Handsel, a CPA in our Accounting Department. A copy
has also been forwarded to Madeline Karpinski, Director of
Human Resources.

Please let me know the course of action you recommend in
terms of departmental reduction by December 31, 2008. We
can meet in person to discuss this if you have any questions
that might not easily be answered via email or telephone.

I will call you next week to follow up on this matter. We can
then determine the best way to proceed.

Letter or Memo of Transmittal

L&L MARKETING
2214 Wacker Ave <> Chicago, IL 60601
Phone 312-555-6699 <> Fax: 312-555-6688

November 24, 2008

(Insert 3 blank lines)

Mr. Malcolm Koslov
917 West Elm Blvd.
Birmingham, MI 48009

(Insert 1 blank line)

Dear Malcolm:

(Insert 1 blank line)

I am enclosing a copy of the report entitled "Marketing
Strategies for Mutual Fund Investments" for your review.
I would like your input on future implementation of these
strategies for all investment firms in the Detroit area.

(Insert 1 blank line)

Since we need to make a decision by January 31, 2009, I
would greatly appreciate a response by January 15, 2009. We
can meet in person to discuss this if you have any questions
that might not easily be answered via email or telephone.

(Insert 1 blank line)

I will call you next week to follow up on this matter. We can
then determine the best way to proceed.

(Insert 1 blank line)

Sincerely,

(Insert 3 blank lines)

Maxwell Claroon
National Accounts Manager

(Insert 1 blank line)

ctl
Enclosure

Letter Format

Table of Contents

- A *table of contents* feature is available on many word processing programs (such as Microsoft Word).

- Titles, chapter titles, main headings, and subheadings can then be added, deleted, or changed readily.

- Use the following guidelines for custom designs:

  1. Use a separate page from the rest of the report.

TABLE OF CONTENTS

(Start 2 inches from the top)

ii

Table of Contents

2. TABLE OF CONTENTS is centered in bold uppercase letters 2 inches from the top of the page.

3. Doublespace, then start the listing of contents.

4. Doublespace between entries and list in sequence.

5. Center entries pertaining to part-titles in uppercase letters.

6. If listing chapters, begin with the chapter number, and then type the title in all uppercase letters. Turnover lines for chapter titles are single spaced.

7. Main headings within chapters are indented from the chapter title in uppercase and lowercase letters. Page numbers are also listed to the right.

Front Matter: Table of Contents

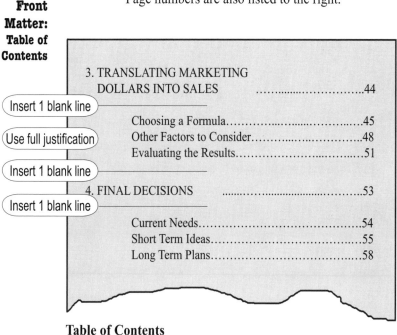

Insert 1 blank line

Use full justification

Insert 1 blank line

Insert 1 blank line

Table of Contents

Lists of Tables or Illustrations

- A *tables and illustrations* feature is available on many word processing programs (such as Microsoft Word). These are convenient for adding, deleting, or changing contents.

- Use the following guidelines for custom designs:

  1. List each table or illustration on a separate page.

  2. TABLES or ILLUSTRATIONS is centered in bold uppercase letters.

  3. Single space entries and doublespace between entries.

  4. Number entries consecutively throughout the document or within each chapter.

**Front Matter:
List of Tables
or Illustrations**

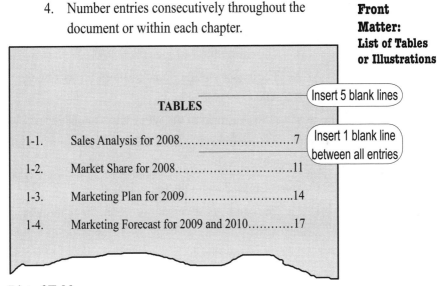

TABLES

Insert 5 blank lines

Insert 1 blank line between all entries

List of Tables

Forewords and Prefaces

- Prefaces are written by the author and forewords are written by someone else.

- Type on a separate page (the foreword precedes the preface if both are used).

- Titles are centered two inches from the top of the page in bold uppercase letters.

- Doublespace after the title and list the text.

- Spacing, indentation, and heading guidelines follow the same as those in the body of the report.

- Forewords must contain the following:

Front Matter: Forewords and Prefaces

  1. The name of the person for whom the report was written.

  2. The reason for the report.

  3. The author's skill or qualifications for writing the report.

  4. An assessment of the author's job on the report.

  5. A request for follow-up action from those receiving the report.

- Prefaces must contain the following:

  1. The name of the person for whom the report was written.

  2. The reason for the report.

  3. The goal of the report.

  4. The topics covered and not covered by the report.

  5. How the data and conclusions were derived.

  6. Acknowledgement of other contributors to the report.

Summaries (also called Executive Summaries)

- Follow the same format guidelines as forewords and prefaces.

- Restrict the length to one page if possible.

Page Numbering

- Number all front matter pages except the title page at the center of the bottom of the page.

- The title page is considered *i*, even though it is not numbered.

- Use lowercase roman numerals (i, ii, iii, iv, v, etc.).

Body

Introduction

- Precedes Chapter 1 (if the book contains chapters).

- INTRODUCTION is centered two inches from the top of the page in bold uppercase letters.

- The first page is considered page 1 of the report.

- If the report contains only one chapter, list INTRODUCTION as a heading, then doublespace between the heading and the text.

- Page numbers are centered at the bottom of the page.

Part-Title Pages

- Part-titles occur when a report contains several chapters organized in parts.

- Insert separate part-title pages directly in front of the chapter that begins each part.

- Use bold uppercase letters.

- Center the text vertically and horizontally.

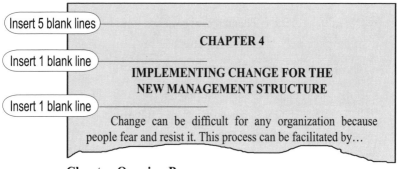

Part-Title Page

Chapter-Opening Pages

Body:
Chapter-
Opening
Page

- Center the chapter number and title on a new page approximately two inches from the top of the page.

- Use bold uppercase letters.

- Begin typing text on the second line below the title.

- If the title is short, it can be typed on the same line as chapter and number.

Chapter-Opening Page

Text Indentation and Spacing

Body:
Text
Indentation
and Spacing

- Check with the proper authority for spacing of business or academic documents. The examples in this book are single spaced.

- Doublespace drafts submitted for evaluation or editing.

- Indent paragraphs 0.5 inch, and leave one blank line between paragraphs.

- Direct quotations four lines or more are single spaced and indented .5 inch from the left and right side margins. Indent the first word an additional .5 inch if the quotation represents the beginning of a paragraph in the original material. Leave one blank line above and below the quotation.

and those observing our employees at work should consider the following email from Mark Haysberg sent on June 17:

> We are considering implementing a change that would let job sharing become a reality. The HR department is working on a procedure for later this year that should result in a win-win for management and employees.

This is a great starting point for employee relations. I think we need to move forward in a positive and proactive manner in order

Text with Direct Long Quotation

Body:
Text
Indentation
and Spacing

- Lists are single spaced with one blank line above and below. Indent .5 inch from the left and right margins, and leave one blank line between each list entry.

We need to ask the following questions before our upcoming infrastructure analysis:

1. Will the investment pay off in the short term or are we expecting the time required to be more than one year?

2. Will the cost exceed the original estimate determined by the committee?

3. What are our major customers expecting in terms of cost increases or decreases?

I strongly suggest we do our homework so that all of these questions can be answered completely.

Text with List

Note: Bullets (circles, triangles, squares, etc.) can also be inserted in place of numbers.

Text Headings

- Limit headings to three levels (not counting the chapter title).

- Make sure all topics are properly represented.

- Use equal amounts of headings in every part of the document.

- Use either complete sentences or phrases for headings. Do not use both in combination since this creates an unparallel structure.

- Three types/styles of headings include:

  - Centered Heads–Center in bold uppercase letters on a line by itself.

  - Side Heads–Flush with left margin in bold uppercase and lowercase letters on a line by itself.

  - Run-in Heads (paragraph headings)–Indent .5 inch from left margin in bold uppercase and lowercase letters (followed by a period); text begins on the same line.

- Leave one blank line above and below every centered or side heading.

Body:
Text
Headings

xxxxxxxxxxxxxxxxxxxxxxxxxxxxxxxxxxxxxxxxxxxxxxxxxxxxx
xxxxxxxxxxxxxxxxxxxxxxxxxxxxxxxxxxxxxxxxxxx.

CENTERED HEAD

Xxxxxxxxxxxxxxxxxxxxxxxxxxxxxxxxxxxxxxxxxxxxxxxxxxxx
xxxxxxxxxxxxxxxxxxxxxxxxxxxxxxxxxx.

Side Head

Run-in Head. Xxxxxxxxxxxxxxxxxxxxxxxxxxxxxxxxxxxxxxx
xxxxxxxxxxxxxxxxxxxxxxxxxxxxxxxxxxxxxxxxxxxxxxxxx.

Run-in Head. Xxxxxxxxxxxxxxxxxxxxxxxxxxxxxxxxxxxxxxx
xxxxxxxxxxxxxxxxxxxxxxxxxxxxxxxxxxxxxxxxxxxxxxx.

Text with Headings

Page Numbering

- If the title and the text start on the same page, then this page is page 1 (using arabic numerals). However, do not put the number on the page itself.

- If the first page is a title page followed by additional pages of front page matter, then number these pages with lowercase roman numerals. The first page following the front matter is page 1 (using arabic numerals). If the first page is a part-title page, then do not number the page, but still count it as page 1.

- Center the page number at the bottom of the page for the first page of every new element in the body or back matter.

- Place the page number in the upper right corner of the page for every other page in the body or back matter.

- If the document is printed on both sides of the paper, then odd numbered pages are on the front side of the paper and even numbered pages are on the back side of the paper.

- If the document is bound, then the even numbered pages are numbered in the upper left margin and the odd numbered pages are numbered in the upper right margin.

- In long documents, separate sequencing of pages can be used within each chapter. For example, chapter one uses 1.1, 1.2, 1.3, etc., and chapter two uses 2.1, 2.2, 2.3, etc.

Back Matter

- Begin each of these on a separate page using the same margins as the body of the report.

Appendices

- Letter each appendix.
- Center APPENDIX, the letter, and the title in bold uppercase letters.
- If the title is short, put APPENDIX, the letter, and the title on the same line.
- If the title is long, use two or more lines and leave one blank line between APPENDIX and the title.
- Leave one blank line between the title and the body.

Back Matter: Appendices

APPENDIX B

RELEVANCE OF WATER ACTIVITY IN COOKED PASTA PRODUCTS AT FDA FOOD ESTABLISHMENTS

Xxxxxxxxxxxxxxxxxxxxxxxxxxxxxxxxxxxxxxxxxxxxxxxxx
xxxxxxxxxxxxxxxxxxxxxxxxxxxxxxxxxxxxxxxxxxxxxxxxx
xxxxxxxxxxxxxxxxxxxxxxxxx

Appendix

Glossaries

Back Matter: Glossaries

- Center GLOSSARY in bold uppercase letters two inches from the top of the page. Leave one blank line before starting the text.
- Use two columns. In the left column, list the terms in alphabetical order using bold uppercase and lowercase letters. In the right column, single space each definition in sentence form, leaving one space between entries.

GLOSSARY

Cyclical perception The idea that perception goes through cycles as people progress through different stages of life.

Standard methods Methods used by the United States Department of Justice to determine factors for crimes committed by various age groups.

Glossary

Manuscripts

In General

- Prepared similar to a report, but written for publication.

- Essentially submitted for articles or books.

- Be certain to ask about specific publisher submission requirements before submitting any manuscript.

Article Manuscripts

- Try to imitate the target publication's format and writing style.

- Use line length equal to that of an average line of copy in the target publication.

- Type one column only per page to allow room for editing in the margins.

- Doublespace to allow room for editing.

- Limit the length of articles to that typically found in the target publication.

- Ask the editor of the publisher for specific requirements pertaining to submission.

Book Manuscripts

Manuscripts:
Book

- Follow the formal report guidelines in regard to headings, spacing, page numbering, and other aspects when writing the front matter, body, and back matter.

- Use 1.5 inches margins to allow room for editing.

- Do not bind the book.

- For special formats, such as large print documents, select a similar book that has been published and adhere to those basic guidelines.

- Be certain to ask about specific publisher submission requirements before submitting any manuscript.

Precautions

- Always retain a duplicate copy of the document in case the material is lost or needs to be discussed with the editor. This copy can be print or electronic, and it is best to keep both if possible.

- Even unpublished manuscripts are automatically copyrighted regardless of their registration with the United States Copyright Office. However, authors might want to contact an attorney for specifics in this matter.

Section Five:
Notes and Bibliography

Footnotes, Endnotes, and Textnotes

- Convey thoughts and ideas that might be distracting if located in the main text.

> [1]Mayor Grace Conardi made this statement regarding the financial condition of the city on September 29, 2008.

- Identify the origin of quotations and citations.

- Use page numbers when referring to a specific page.

> [2]Jason Wilson, *Rebuilding Classic Automobiles*, rev. ed., Harper Row, Boston, 2007, p. 224.

Footnotes

- *Footnotes* are sometimes preferred over *endnotes* or *textnotes* because all pertinent information is available on the same page.

- A superscripted arabic numeral in text represents a word, sentence, phrase, or quotation.

- The superscripted arabic numeral in text should appear as close as possible to the word, sentence, phrase, or quotation that it represents, but it is sometimes best to place it at the end of the sentence to minimize confusion.

> *Acceptable*
> Jamie Simonti's most recent book, *Walking with International Superstars: Life as a Professional Sports Agent*,[1] was published over three years ago.
>
> *Preferable*
> Jamie Simonti's most recent book, *Walking with International Superstars: Life as a Professional Sports Agent*, was published over three years ago.[1]

- The superscripted numbers in text run consecutively throughout the document or start new with each chapter.
- There is no space between the superscripted arabic numeral in text and the word, sentence, phrase, or quotation. Superscripted numbers are placed after all punctuation marks except a dash (they precede a dash).

University research indicates middle school students' social skills are influenced by family more than peers.[1]

Maximilian Periwinkle's study titled, "New Discoveries in the Nurture and Nature Debate" supports the twin's behavior.[2]

This thinking is derived from the article "Surviving Undercover Life in a Bronx Street Gang"[3]–which was written by a former CIA agent.

Footnotes

- Place corresponding entries at the foot (or bottom) of the page where the source is referenced in text.
- Entries at the bottom of a page must correspond with reference numbers in text.
- If text runs short on a page (such as at the end of a chapter), still place the entry at the bottom of the page.
- If an entry is too long for one page, it should be completed at the bottom of the next page (with no indent or identification on the next page).
- A two inch horizontal line is placed between the text and the first entry at the bottom of the page. Doublespace between the text and horizontal line, and doublespace between the horizontal line and the first entry.
- Indent the first line of each entry at the bottom of the page .5 inch from the left margin. The following lines are flush with the left margin.
- Single space each entry at the bottom of the page, and doublespace between entries.

- A *footnote* feature is available on many word processing programs (such as Microsoft Word). This software automatically positions footnotes at the bottom of the page, inserts the horizontal line to separate the notes from the text above, and numbers each entry. However, these programs might result in footnotes differing from the example below (there might be no indent of the first footnote, no space between the horizontal line and first footnote, and no extra space between footnotes). This method is acceptable in many instances, but check with the proper authority when writing any type of business or academic document.

In the military, publicly berating a subordinate in order to achieve positive behavioral change is accepted.[1] A boot camp drill sergeant, for example, may scream at a new recruit and call him or her derogatory names because his or her bed was not made properly. This type of verbal abuse would probably not be accepted if a hotel manager were to reprimand a maid in a similar manner for the same infraction.[2]

Footnotes

[1]Anthony J. Borannis, *Argumentative Strategies in the Military*, 4th ed., Sinclair Books, Chicago, 2008, p. 112.

[2]Margaret Lagravis, *Hotel Etiquette: A Training Guide for Management*, Leodan Books, New York, 2008, p. 24.

- Multiple footnotes within the same paragraph of text can combine all of the information in one note (if this can be done without confusion). Place the superscripted arabic numeral after the last reference in text.

Information overload is analyzed from an organizational perspective by Annette Haggerty, Kenneth Watson, and Victoria Maceroni.[1]

[1] Annette Haggerty, *Organizational Solutions*, Wilson Books, Chicago, 2008, p.12; Kenneth G. Watson, *Workplace Change*, Farwell, New York, 2007, p. 233; and Victoria Ann Maceroni, *Symptoms of Organizational Decline*, Warner-Fess Books, 3rd ed., Baltimore, 2007, p. 131.

Endnotes

Endnotes

- Endnotes are sometimes preferred over footnotes because they leave pages looking less cluttered.

- A superscripted arabic numeral in text represents a word, sentence, phrase, or quotation.

- The superscripted arabic numeral in text should appear as close as possible to the word, sentence, phrase, or quotation that it represents, but it is sometimes best to place it at the end of the sentence to minimize confusion. See the *Footnote* section for an example.

- The superscripted numbers in text run consecutively throughout the document or start new with each chapter.

- There is no space between the superscripted arabic numeral in text and the word, sentence, phrase, or quotation unless a dash is involved (superscripted numbers precede a dash). See the *Footnote* section for an example.

- Place corresponding entries on a separate *Notes* page at the end of a chapter or end of a document.

- Entries on the notes page must correspond with reference numbers in text.

- The notes page contains the heading NOTES, which is centered in bold uppercase letters and placed two inches from the top of the page.

- Leave two blank lines between the heading and the first entry on the notes page.

- Indent the first line of each entry on the notes page .5 inch from the left margin. The following lines are flush with the left margin.

- Single space each entry on the notes page, and doublespace between entries.

- If a document contains only one chapter, then the endnotes can begin on the same page that the text ends. Leave three blank lines before the NOTES heading and two blank lines after it (before the first entry). This method is acceptable in many instances, but it is not as common as a separate notes page. Check with the proper authority when writing any type of business or academic document.

Endnotes

- If a document contains multiple chapters and endnotes are listed for each chapter, then an appropriate heading (chapter 1, chapter 2, etc.) should be listed above each

NOTES

1. Art Kerkau and Carol Creisher, *Changing Times on Kingston Avenue*, Axel & Joyce, Huntington Woods, Mich., 2008, pp. 29–31.

2. Lucy M. Gainsworth, "Change and Suburban Neighborhoods: A Qualitative Analysis," *Change Management*, Vol. 27, No. 4, June 2008, pp. 175–182.

3. Ibid., p. 181.

4. D'Andre Sims, "Suburban Renewal: Inside a Conservative Bedroom Community," *Newsweek*, July 2008, pp. 22–29.

Leave a 2-inch top margin

Leave 2 blank lines

Doublespace between entries

Notes Page

series of entries. The heading is placed at the left margin in uppercase and lowercase bold letters (with two blank lines above and one blank line below).

Endnotes

- Multiple endnotes within the same paragraph of text can combine all of the information in one note (if this can be done without confusion). Place the superscripted arabic numeral after the last reference. See the *Footnote* section for an example.

- An *endnote* feature is available on many word processing programs (such as Microsoft Word). This software automatically positions endnotes at the end of the document, inserts a horizontal line to separate the notes from the text above, and numbers each entry. This method is acceptable in many instances, but check with the proper authority when writing any type of business or academic document.

Textnotes

Textnotes

- Textnotes can be used for reports that have no bibliography and only a few source references. They can also be used in reports that have a complete bibliography *and* a number of source references.

- Textnotes are sometimes preferred over footnotes because they leave pages looking less cluttered.

- List the author's surname and page number.

- Place citations in parentheses within the text to provide an abbreviated reference that is later detailed in a bibliography section.

In text

This evolved from the liberal notion that every individual should claim the land as his or her own (Pottsboro, p. 171).

or

Pottsboro (p. 171) noted that this evolved from the liberal notion that every individual should claim the land as his or her own.

Bibliography (Business Style)

Pottsboro, Milton Raymond, *The Evolution of American Thought*, 2d ed., Jarred-Baldori, Dodgeville, Wis., 2008.

- Sometimes the *p.* and *pp.* are omitted (and no comma is used). For example, the Pottsboro citation would be (Pottsboro 171), but omitting the *p.* or *pp.* is not the most common method. Check with the proper authority when writing any type of business or academic document.

Textnotes

- Multiple citations by the same author use a publication year or abbreviated title (if publication years are the same) for differentiation. The abbreviated title is a key word or phrase.

If publication years are different
(Kapress, 2007, p. 212)
(Kapress, 2005, p. 113)
If publication years are the same
(Kapress, *Age*, p. 212)
(Kapress, *Race*, p. 113)

- Multiple citations by authors with the same surname list the first initial in addition to the surname.

> The documents were deemed unrelated to the case (L. Perkins, p. 27). However, certain court situations warrant the need for information that might not appear to have linkage (P. Perkins, p. 109).

- A document with only a few sources can list the complete source data in the parenthetical textnotes, thereby eliminating the need for a bibliography. However, this is not the most common method, so check with the proper authority when writing any type of business or academic document.

Textnotes

> One such invention involved using household tablespoons for transmission of heat. This proved to be critical for thermal processing in many industrial manufacturers (Larry Schavey, *Thermal Solutions*, Random House, Chicago, 2007, p. 143).

- If entries are sequentially numbered in a bibliography, citations in text may list the source using the appropriate entry number (along with the page reference).

- This is not the most common method, so check with the proper authority when writing any type of business or academic document.

> These findings are based on the research of several independent laboratories throughout the United States and Canada (17, p. 314).

Online Sources

Online Sources

- List URLs and email addresses.

> *URL*
> http://www.elmorefarms.com
>
> *Email address*
> jackhartsig@hotmail.com

- Attempt to fit URLs and email addresses on one line, but if they will not fit on one line use the following guidelines:
    - Do not insert hyphens in URLs or email addresses to signify line breaks.
    - Break URLs after double slashes (//) that mark the end of a protocol.
    - Break URLs before dots (.), hyphens (-), underlines (_), single dashes (–), single slashes (/), or other marks of punctuation.
    - Break emails before the *at* (@) symbol or before the dot (.).

URL acceptable first line	URL acceptable next line
http://	www.countrysmokehouse.com
http://www.udm	.english.edu
http://www.house.gov	/_smith
http://www.temper	-Johnson.com
Email acceptable first line	*Email acceptable next line*
summer1969	@earthlink.net
donald	.francis@midvalley.com

- Enclose URLs and email addresses in angle brackets (< >) in footnotes, endnotes, and bibliographies. Convert to a hyperlink if the document is for posting online or emailing (so the site or email can be clicked for instant access). Do not convert to a hyperlink if the document is for print copy.

- List publication dates and access dates.

[1]LaDonna Marquis, "Exploring Northern Minnesota in the Winter," *Boston Times Online*, May 6, 2008, <www.bostimes.com/2008/edt/out/34.html>, accessed on June 21, 2008.

Books (Business Style)

- List author(s), title (italicized), publisher, publication place, publication year, and page number (if applicable). Page numbers are not listed if the book is being referred to as a whole.

- Titles are capitalized headline style.

- Headline style means the first and last words and all nouns, pronouns, adjectives, verbs and adverbs (for titles and subtitles) must be capitalized. Use lowercase for articles (*a, an, the*), coordinating conjunctions (*and, for, nor, but, or, so*), and prepositions (*to, toward, with, under*, etc.), unless they are the first or last word of a title or subtitle. Use lowercase for the words *to* and *as* at all times.

Books:
Business
Style

[1]Terry McClaren, *Football Heroes as Boyfriends*, Hickory College Press, Delphos, Kans., 2008.

- Elements identified in text do not need to be repeated in notes.

William Nicol, in his book *Modern Concepts in Pest Control Application*, discusses "selective spider breeding" as one potential solution to the growing fly infestation problem.[2]

[2] Macomb House, Chicago, 2008, p. 117.

- The preferred way to handle a long quotation (four lines or longer) is to indent it a half inch from each side margin. The actual quotation should be single-spaced. Do not enclose it in quotation marks; the indentation implies that it is a direct quotation. A blank line should be left above and below the quotation.

While it is not certain what transpired during that revolutionary period, a sense of despair could be sensed within the troops. The war was said to be lost before the final battles were ever fought:

> For the most part, everyone had given up. The excitement that arose from the initial attempts at fighting for a better life was now gone. Positive thinking had all but disappeared as the men sat motionless waiting for their next orders. This seemed strange since there was no official word of surrender, but the troops could not help becoming engulfed in the negative atmosphere that abounded. With at least two more battles on the horizon, the situation appeared hopeless.[3]

[3]James P. LeBoeuf, *Realities of War*, 4th ed., Thompson-Cain, Los Angeles, 2008, p. 316.

**Books:
Business
Style**

Books (Academic Style)

- List author(s), title (italicized), publication place, publisher, publication year (in parentheses), and page numbers (if applicable). Page numbers are not listed if the book is being referred to as a whole.

- Authors are listed by first name, middle name or initial (if applicable), and surname.

- Titles are capitalized headline style.

**Books:
Academic
Style**

[4]Sandra Frankowski and Lori Lofton, *Vegetarian Recipes for Carnivores* (St. Clair Shores, Mich.: Butcher Boy Books, 2008), p. 214.

The following examples of books utilize the *Business Style* methodology, but these can be converted to the *Academic Style* by simply altering the publication information.

Books with Editions

Books: Editions

- Common abbreviations are as follows:

Second Edition	*is listed as*	2d ed.
Third Edition	*is listed as*	3d ed.
Fourth Edition	*is listed as*	4th ed.
Revised Edition	*is listed as*	rev. ed.

- List author(s), title (italicized), edition (if not the first), publisher, publication place, publication year, and page numbers (if applicable).

[5]Paul Dewitt and Gary Runwhip, *Chess Strategies Made Simple*, 3d ed., Pinto Books, Wooster, Ohio, 2007, p. 79.

Books with Subtitles

Books: Subtitles

- List author(s), title (italicized), subtitle (italicized), edition (if not the first), publisher, publication place, publication year, page numbers (if applicable).

- Separate the title and the subtitle with a colon, and capitalize the first word after the colon (even if it would normally not be capitalized).

[6] Kendall Gladstone and Scott McClintock, *Working Toward a Common Goal: Our Friendship at the Warren Racquetball Center*, Barker State College Press, Boston, 2008.

Books with Volume Numbers and Volume Titles

Books: Volumes

- List author(s), title (italicized), volume number, volume title (italicized), edition (if not the first), publisher, publication place, publication year, page numbers (if applicable).

- Use *Vol.* to abbreviate *Volume*.

[7]Latrell Emerson Shackelford, *The History of Physics in Canada*, Vol. 1, *The Industrial Revolution*, 4th ed., Lewis & Mingelhoff, Toronto, 2007, pp. 614–738.

Books with Volume Numbers, but No Volume Titles

Books:
Volumes

- List author(s) or editor(s), title (italicized), edition (if not the first), publisher, publication place, publication year, volume number, page numbers (if applicable).

> [8]Sterling Thompson (ed.), *Microbiology of Acidic Foods*, 3d ed., Zerelli Science, Westminster, Md., 2007, Vol. 4, pp. 544–559.

Note: The above example uses an editor instead of an author. In this case the editor is listed in place of the author.

Chapter References from Books by One Author

Books:
Chapter
References

- List author(s), title (italicized), publisher, publication place, publication year, chapter number, chapter title (in quotation marks, if applicable), page numbers (if applicable).

- Use *Chap.* to abbreviate *Chapter.*

> [9]Milton Voggles, *Birth of an Empire: The Junge Furniture Company,* Hargrove Books, Pittsburgh, 2008, Chap. 3, "Metal Replaces Wood," pp. 254–271.

Selections from Collected Works and Selections from Anthologies

Books:
Anthologies

- List author(s), title of selection (in quotation marks), title (italicized), publisher, publication place, publication year, and page numbers.

> [10]Walter Hess, "Window of Opportunity," *The Last Great American Salesman,* Herman & Merle, New York, 2007, pp. 21–46.

Selections from Anthologies in Books

Books: Anthologies

- List author(s) of selection, title of selection (in quotation marks), editor of anthology, title (italicized), publisher, publication place, publication year, and page numbers.

> [11]Marley Wales, "Managerial Incompetence," in Ted Rockett (ed.), *Subliminal Thinking of Corporate America*, Domanski Books, Exeter, R.I., 2007, pp. 212–244.

Articles in Referenced Books

Books: Articles

- Referenced books contain established facts (dictionaries, encyclopedias, record books, etc.)

- List author(s) [if available], article title (in quotation marks), referenced work title (italicized), edition (if not the first), publisher (if not well known), publication place (if not well known), publication year, volume number, and page numbers (if applicable).

> [12]Carl M. Reiter, "Public School Boards," *Tower Encyclopedia of Education*, 8th ed., 2008.
>
> [13]"Organic Meat," *Dictionary of Organic Foods*, 2d ed., Nikki & Helms, Afton, Tenn., 2007, Vol. 4, p. 312.

Quotations from Secondary Sources in Books

Books: Secondary Sources

- Always use the original source if possible.

- List original source author(s), title (italicized), publisher, place, date, page numbers (if applicable), *quoted by* or *cited by* author, title (italicized), publisher, place, date, and page numbers.

> [14]Frederick T. Hibbard and Maurice Allen Rosella, *Power Selling*, Simon & Leeman, New York, 2007, p. 317, cited by Luis Reynoso, *Profitable Sales,* Cronin Books, Chicago, 2008, p. 69.

Online Books

- Follow the printed book guidelines and add the URL and access date.

Online
Books

> [1]Lucinda Ellis, *Indian Tribes of Western Montana*, Johnson & Mills, Chicago, 2006, p. 181, <http:// www.montana.indianbooks.edu /native.html4388>, accessed on August 15, 2008.

- Publication information is omitted if it is not available (which sometimes happens with books that are only available online). Use *n.d.* in place of the publication date if missing.

> [2]Dennis Willet, *Spices of the Western World*, n.d., <http://www.spices.west.com/native.html6312>, accessed October 22, 2008.

Newspaper Articles

- List author(s) [if available], article title (in quotation marks), newspaper name (italicized), date, section number, page numbers (if applicable), and column (if applicable).

Newspaper
Articles

- Elements identified in text do not need to be repeated in notes. See *Books (Business Style)* for an example.

> [1]Angela Winkeleford, "Failing to Plan Results in Planning to Fail," *The Boston Globe*, June 21, 2008, Sec. C, p. 3, col. 1.

Online Newspaper Articles

- List author(s) [if available], article title (in quotation marks), newspaper name (italicized), date, URL, access date.

Online
Newspaper
Articles

Online Newspaper Articles

[2]Karen Ann Hengstecki, "Discovering the Fountain of Youth," *The Montana Press Online*, March 13, 2008, <http://www.montanapress.com/2008/5 /home/comment.html>, accessed on May 4, 2008.

[3]"Know Your Children's Friends," *The Hartford Journal Online*, May 7, 2009, <http://hartfordpress.com /2009/6/family.html>, accessed on June 12, 2009.

Magazine Articles

Magazine Articles

- List author(s) [if available], article title (in quotation marks), magazine name (italicized), date, and page numbers (if applicable).

- Omit comma between article title and magazine title if title ends with an exclamation point or a question mark.

- Elements identified in text do not need to be repeated in notes. See *Books (Business Style)* for an example.

[1]Trevor Williams, "High School Basketball in the Florida Panhandle," *Amateur Sports*, March 2008, pp. 17–21.

[2]Valerie M. Pokowski, "What Makes a True Conservative?" *American Politics*, November-December 2007, pp. 54–58.

Online Magazine Articles

Online Magazine Articles

- List author(s) [if available], article title (in quotation marks), magazine name (italicized), date, URL, access date.

[3]Katie PaKelts, "Cross Breeding Pure Breeds," *Dog Breeding Online*, June 14, 2008, <http://www.dogbreeding.com /pure/column.html7445>, accessed on September 29, 2008.

Journal Articles

- List author(s), article title (in quotation marks), journal title (italicized), series number (if applicable), volume number (if applicable), issue number (if applicable), date, and page numbers (if applicable).

- Journal titles may be abbreviated if they are familiar to the intended readers or they are identified in the bibliography.

- Use *Vol.* to abbreviate *Volume.*

- Use *No.* to abbreviate *Number.*

> [1]Harvey Wallbanger, "The Influence of Alcohol Consumption on Social Relationships," *Conceptual Sociology*, Vol. 14, No. 2, June 2008, pp. 19–26.

CD-ROMs

- List author(s) [if available], article title (in quotation marks), title of CD-ROM (italicized), CD-ROM and version (in parentheses, if applicable), publisher (may be omitted), publication place (may be omitted), publication year, and locator reference (if applicable).

- Examples of locator references include paragraph numbers or page numbers (if applicable).

> [1]Robert Chambers and Arthur J. Peters, "Tumbling Under Warm Temperatures," *Meat Processing Technology in Europe* (CD-ROM Version 2), Cincinnati State Univ. Press, Cincinnati, 2008, p. 244.

Pamphlets, Newsletters, or Bulletins

- List author(s) [if available], article title (in quotation marks), publication title (italicized), series title and series number (if applicable), volume number and issue number (if applicable), sponsoring organization, place, date, and page numbers.

Pamphlets

- Sponsoring organizations may be omitted if incorporated in the title of the publication.
- Add the URL to the listing for online versions.

[1]Frederick Wayne Porkerhouse, "Suburban Chicago," *Municipal Parks in Illinois*, Vol. 21, No. 4, National Park Service, Washington, June 2008, p. 67.

Unpublished Theses or Dissertations

- List author, title (in quotation marks), identifying phrase (*doctoral dissertation* or *master's thesis*), academic institution, place, date, and page numbers.

Unpublished Theses

[1]Cynthia L. Helmacki, "Socialization and Job Status: A Quantitative Study in a Vending Machine Repair Facility," doctoral dissertation, Wayne State University, Detroit, 2007, pp. 198–211.

Online Unpublished Theses or Dissertations

- Follow the printed guidelines for *Unpublished Theses or Dissertations*, and add the URL.

[1]Cynthia L. Helmacki, "Socialization and Job Status: A Quantitative Study in a Vending Machine Repair Facility," doctoral dissertation, Wayne State University, Detroit, 2007, p. 28, <http//www.umi.com/diss/soc/wayneu/pubno449603248>.

Interviews or Personal Conversations

Interviews

- List name of person interviewed (and title or affiliation if appropriate), *personal interview* (if face-to-face or list *telephone conversation*), and interview date.

[1]Marcello Pilliano (professor of anthropology, Hartford College), personal interview, May 5, 2008.

Interviews Conducted by Others

- List name of person interviewed (and title or affiliation if appropriate), *interviewed by* name, and interview date.

> [2]Manny McGuire (professor of anthropology, Colorado State University), interviewed by Edward Schneider, March 14, 2008.

Radio or Television Interviews

- List name of person interviewed, *interviewed by* name of interviewer, program (in quotations) or series title (italicized), radio station or television channel, and broadcast date.

> [3]Winfred Manchester, interviewed by Alysha Eckert, *English Ancestry Series*, WCRX, June 2, 2008.

Speeches

- List speaker (and title or affiliation if appropriate), title of speech (in quotation marks), *speech given at* type of meeting (convention, conference, symposium), place, and date.

> [1]Christopher DeVario (Emerson Music), "Roots of Jazz Music," speech given at National Association of Jazz Musicians Convention, New Orleans, July 9, 2008.

Papers Presented at Meetings

- List speaker(s), title of paper (in quotation marks), *paper presented at* type of meeting (convention, conference, symposium), place, and date.

> [1]Steven Sandusky, "The Reality of Freedom," paper presented at the National Firearms Society Conference, Taylorsville, Utah, September 13, 2007.

Reports

Reports

- List author(s), title of report (in quotation marks), author's sponsoring organization or company, place, date, and page numbers.

> [1]Nicholas Woehnker and Daniel Dandurand, "Factors in Frozen Food Technology," Dilmore Foods, Montréal, January 17, 2008, pp. 22–31.

Memos or Letters

- List author, subject line (in quotation marks), document type (*memo* or *letter*), and date.

Memos or Letters

> [1]Ronald Olsen, "Second Thoughts on the BSL Merger," letter, April 6, 2008.

Memos or Letters Addressed to Other People

- List author, subject line (in quotation marks), document type (*memo* or *letter*), *addressed to* recipient name, and date.

> [2]Felipe Peredez, "SSOP Standards at Alexander & Hornung," memo, addressed to Gabriella Morantez, June 13, 2008.

Email

- List author, subject line (in quotation marks), *email message*, and date.

Email

- The email address may be added in parentheses if it ends with the name of an organization.

- Do not provide personal email addresses without the owner's permission.

[1]Kenneth Lawson, "Sales and Marketing Preparation for 2008," e-mail message, December 17, 2007.

[2]Shelby Harp (shelby.harp@bageltown.com), "Inventory Control Procedures for the Fort Wayne Stores," e-mail message, January 12, 2008.

Internet Forum, Listserv, or Newsgroup Messages

- List author, author's email (in angle brackets, if appropriate), subject line (in quotation marks), posting date, message URL or email (in angle brackets, if appropriate), and access date.

- The email address may be added in parentheses if it ends with the name of an organization.

- Do not provide personal email addresses without the owner's permission.

[1]National Communication Center <ncc.info@cmt.gov>, "New Cell Phone Technology," August 14, 2008, <http://listserve.cmt.gov/cgi.bin=p&f=305>, accessed on September 1, 2008.

[2]Marley Talbot, "Credit Card Rebates," August 26, 2008, <internetscams@yahoogroups.com>, accessed on November 13, 2008.

Elements of Notes

Author Names

- List authors' names in the same order as they appear in the reference.

- Use *and* (not *&*) to separate authors.

- Titles (Ph.D., M.D., J.D., etc.) are not listed.

[1]Shannon Kelp, *Secrets of Successful Restaurateurs: Results Based on Experience*, Jenson-Tyne, New York, 2008, pp. 23–31.

[2]Michael T. Kirsch and Sharon F. Carl, "Sanitation Standards of Dairy Farms: Are Pathogens a Public Concern?" *Journal of Dairy Safety*, Vol. 11, No. 3, July 2007, pp. 233–251.

[3]Victoria Gutinelli with Jerome Beal, *Human Resource Challenges Facing Corporate America*, 4th ed., Parker-Rolloff, Miami, 2008, p. 149.

[4]M. J. Bollas, *Dancing with Heroes: Life as a Power Broker in Computer Hardware*, Harman Books, Chicago, 2007, p. 29.

[5]Andrew Kent Werling, Jr. and William P. Eisel, *Changes in Metal Detection Design*, 2d ed., Markem Books, Picture Rocks, Pa., 2007, pp. 212–231.

- Repeat surnames for authors with the same surname.

[6]Jennifer M. Summers and Jacqueline P. Summers (eds.), *Psychological Terms Made Easy*, Brookings, Baltimore, 2007, p. 112.

- Use *et al.* after the first author's name when three or more authors are listed.

[7]Violet Splatt et al., *Automated Mailing Systems For Law Firms*, McGraw-Homes, Lander, Wyo., 2008.

- List organizations in place of authors if necessary.

> [8]National Forestry Association, *Forest Fire Prevention*, Apple Books, Las Vegas, 2008, p. 26.

- If the organization is the author and the publisher, list it only once (as the publisher).

> [9]*Gun Safety at Home*, American Firearms Association, Bernice, Okla., 2007, pp. 12–13.

- If there are editors but no authors, list the editors (*ed.*) or (*eds.*).
- The city does not need to be listed if it is in the publisher name, well known, and not confused with another city of the same name.

Elements of Notes: Author Names

> [10]Donald M. Glicker (ed.), *History of Michigan Elementary Schools*, Univ. of Detroit Press, 2005.
>
> [11]James Kailukaitis and Russell Chiesa, Jr. (eds.), *History of Michigan Middle Schools*, rev. ed., Univ. of Detroit Press, 2007.
>
> [12]Denise Dejorde et al. (eds.), *History of Michigan High Schools*, 3d ed., Univ. of Detroit Press, 2008.

- Omit editor names in reference works (dictionaries, encyclopedias, directories, etc.) that have no authors.

> [13]*Dictionary of British Folk Legends*, Talbot Univ. Press, London, 2008, Vol. 3, p. 244.

- If work has no author or editor, list title in place of author. Do not use *Anonymous*.

> [14]*Panthers of Southern Florida*, Bookish-Hillman, Bartow, Fla., 2007, p. 23.

Publisher Names

- Omit publisher names from newspapers and other periodicals.

- Publishers' names may be listed as they appear in the work, or they can be abbreviated. However, the chosen method must be used consistently throughout. If in doubt, do not abbreviate.

Elements of Notes: Publisher Names

- The following are examples of abbreviations:

Full Name	Acceptable Abbreviation
Beth L. Fassine	Fassine
Joseph Trumsett & Sons	Trumsett
Chapelka House, Inc.	Chapelka House
Peckell Press	Peckell
Lang-Thulride Company	Lang-Thulride
Thomas Education Company	Thomas
OttoMarwell Publishers	OttoMarwell
Piper Companies, LLC	Piper
Bucknell, Gilroy, and Company	Bucknell, Gilroy
Alcorn State University Press	Alcorn State Univ. Press
University of Pennsylvania Press	Univ. of Pennsylvania Press
Lanigan & Mueller	No acceptable abbreviation
Hanus, Sapine, and Masters	No acceptable abbreviation

Publication Places

- List by the city only, unless that city is not well known or can be confused with another city of the same name.

Elements of Notes: Publication Places

- List lesser known or same name cities with the state (and province or country if applicable).

- Omit the place of publication from periodical entries.

Examples of Cities Where No State or Country is Necessary			
Boston	New York	Chicago	Baltimore
Munich	Toronto	London	France

Examples of Cities Where State, Province, or Country is Necessary

Cambridge, Mass.	Lander, Wyo.	Gilford, N.H.
Owosso, Mich.	Weimar, Germany	Barrie, Ontario
Cambridge, England	Clichy, France	

- State abbreviations (other than those used in addresses) are as follows:

Alabama	Ala.	Nevada	Nev.
Arizona	Ariz.	New Hampshire	N.H.
Arkansas	Ark.	New Jersey	N.J.
California	Calif.	New Mexico	N. Mex.
Canal Zone	C.Z.	New York	N.Y.
Colorado	Colo.	North Carolina	N.C.
Connecticut	Conn.	North Dakota	N. Dak.
Delaware	Del.	Oklahoma	Okla.
District of Columbia	D.C.	Oregon	Oreg.
Florida	Fla.	Pennsylvania	Pa.
Georgia	Ga.	Puerto Rico	P.R.
Illinois	Ill.	Rhode Island	R.I.
Indiana	Ind.	South Carolina	S.C.
Kansas	Kans.	South Dakota	S. Dak.
Kentucky	Ky.	Tennessee	Tenn.
Louisiana	La.	Texas	Tex.
Maryland	Md.	Vermont	Vt.
Massachusetts	Mass.	Virgin Islands	V.I.
Michigan	Mich.	Virginia	Va.
Minnesota	Minn.	Washington	Wash.
Mississippi	Miss.	West Virginia	W. Va.
Missouri	Mo.	Wisconsin	Wis.
Montana	Mont.	Wyoming	Wyo.

Elements of Notes: Publication Places

Note: Alaska, Guam, Hawaii, Idaho, Iowa, Maine, Ohio, and Utah are spelled out completely (no abbreviation).

Some organizations and institutions favor abandoning the above abbreviations in favor of two-letter abbreviations. Check with the proper authority when writing any type of business or academic document.

Elements of Notes: Publication Places

- Do not abbreviate *Mount, Point, Port* or *Fort.*

Mount Pleasant	Point Pelee	Port Austin	Fort Wayne

- Abbreviate *Saint* in United States place names.

St. Louis	St. Charles River	St. Paul Cathedral

Page Numbers

- Use *p.* for one page and *pp.* for multiple pages.
- Use page numbers when referring to a specific page.

Elements of Notes: Page Numbers

Reference	Pages Referred To
p. 6	6
pp. 237–294	237 to 294
pp. 428 f.	428 and the following page
pp. 319 ff.	319 and the following pages

Note: Avoid using *f.* and *ff.* whenever possible.

Some organizations and institutions favor abandoning the *p.* and *pp.* when listing page numbers. Check with the proper authority when writing any type of business or academic document.

Subsequent References

Elements of Notes: Subsequent References

- References to work identified in immediately preceding footnotes or endnotes may be shortened with *Ibid. Ibid.* replaces all the information in the previous note that would otherwise have been carried over.

> [1]Kathy Sieloff, *Gumby and Pokey as Learning Tools for Children*, Palomino Books, Warren, Mich., 2008, p. 27.
>
> [2]Ibid., p. 34–*Ibid.* represents all information except the page number
>
> [3]Ibid.–*Ibid.* represents all information

- References to work identified in earlier (but not immediately preceding) footnotes or endnotes may be shortened using the author's surname(s) and page numbers (if applicable).

> *Initial reference*
>
> [4]Wesley Zelniak, *Modern Day Communism*, Univ. of Schaefer Press, Munich, 2008, p. 147.
>
> *Subsequent reference (not immediately following)*
>
> [11]Zelniak, p. 217.

Note: Add a bibliography when using short forms for subsequent references so readers can quickly find the complete reference in alphabetical order.

- Subsequent references to work from different authors with the same surname list initials in addition to surnames.

> [12]Jeremy J. Wilson, *Computer Programs for Automotive Suppliers*, Wilkerson Books, New York, 2008, p. 225.
>
> [13]Michele Wilson, *Automotive Technology in Western Europe*, Milford State Univ. Press, Gilford, N.H., 2007, p. 11.
>
> [19]J. J. Wilson, p. 261.
>
> [20]M. Wilson, p. 102.

- List the authors, shortened titles, and page numbers when referring to subsequent works by the same author(s).

- If referring to an article in a periodical, list the periodical title rather than the article title.

Elements of
Notes:
Subsequent
References

[21]Thomas Nanz, *Winning Dodgeball Strategies*, Challenge Books, Baltimore, 2007, p. 19.

[22]Thomas Nanz, *Winning Football Strategies*, Challenge Books, Baltimore, 2006, p. 92.

[25]Nanz, *Dodgeball*, p. 58.

[27]Nanz, *Football*, p. 214.

Bibliographies

In General

- Place at the end of a report.

- Lists all works consulted in preparation and all works cited in notes.

- Contains the same information and order as footnote and endnote entries. The differences are the order of the author's names (entries are not in the same order) and the page numbers.

Business Style

- Place at the end of the document.

Bibliographies:
Business Style

- List the heading BIBLIOGRAPHY (bold uppercase letters) at the top of the page (centered, two inches from the top of the page). Leave two lines between the heading and the first entry.

- List all entries in alphabetical order by first author's surname (inverted), followed by the other author's names (not inverted).

- Entries without authors are listed alphabetically by editors, organizations, or titles. Ignore *A, An* and *The* at the beginning of titles when alphabetizing.

BIBLIOGRAPHY

Anderson, Darnell Henry (ed.), *Grandparents Giving Birth*, Geo-Clemmens Books, Boston, 2007.

Delina, Maria, "Realities of Older Parenthood," *Journal of Family Education*, Vol. 4, No. 1, June 2007, pp. 217–243.

Esmoretta, Janice, et al., *Pregnant at Forty*, Protter Books, Chicago, 2008.

A Guide to a Healthy Older Pregnancy, North Carolina Physical Health Group, Raleigh, 2008.

Krebelle, Cheryl, "Exposing Medical Thinking about Women: Biological Clock or Biological Crock?" *Health Science Quarterly*, Vol. 1, No. 2, January 2008, pp. 312–326.

———, "Reanalyzing Pregnancy in Older Women," *Health Science Quarterly,* Vol. 6, No. 1, June 2008, pp. 11–29.

1,000 Reasons Women Can Get Pregnant after Age 35, Beckwell Pregnancy Committee, New York, 2007.

Rocheldo, Gregory, "Conservative Aspects of Medical Leadership in the United States," *Medical Monographs*, Vol. 2, 2007, pp. 312–331.

St. John, David P. and Michael L. Mondrella, "Advancements in Medical X-Ray Design," *Medical Science Technology*, July-August 2008, pp. 219–228.

Bibliographies: Business Style

Bibliography–Business Style

- Use a long dash (three-em dash) to replace the author(s) for multiple entries by the same author(s). List the works by that author alphabetically by title.

- List page numbers if the entry is part of a larger work such as an article or chapter.

- Use *et al.* after the first author's name when three or more authors are listed.

- Entries beginning with a number are alphabetical as if the number were spelled out.

- Set the left and right margins at 1 inch.

- The first line of each entry is flush with the left margin, and all subsequent lines are indented .5 inch.

Bibliographies: Business Style

- Single space entries with double spacing between each entry.

- Entries do not need to be numbered. However, if entries are sequentially numbered (using the *textnote* system described earlier), then citations in text list the source using the appropriate entry number (along with the page reference).

- Type the number at the left margin of the bibliography, then leave a space and type the entry so that every line begins under the first letter of the first word in the line above.

In-Text

These results are based on research conducted under controlled conditions (16, p. 241).

Bibliography

16. Norand Charles, "Psychological Factors Affecting Cat Welfare in Animal Shelters," *Veterinary Quarterly*, Vol. 12, No. 2, July 2008.

Numbered Bibliography

Note: This is not the most common method, so check with the proper authority when writing any type of business or academic document.

Academic Style

- Periods follow the authors (editors or organizations), titles, and publishing information.
- Set the left and right margins at 1 inch.
- The first line of each entry is indented .5 inch from the left margin, and all subsequent lines are flush with the left margin.
- Parentheses normally used to enclose the publishing information for footnotes and endnotes are omitted.
- The heading is bold and all uppercase letters.

Bibliographies: Academic Style

BIBLIOGRAPHY

Letton, Suzanne Marie. *Hot on the Grill.* Harlingen, Tex.: Fuscinelli Books, 2008.

National Charcoal Association. *Grilling for Greatness,* 3d ed. Chicago: Prestwick Books, 2007.

Bibliography–Academic Style

Section Six:
Tables

In General

- The *table* feature of many word processors can be used, but be careful because these programs do have some limitations.

- Leave one blank row at the top and one blank row at the bottom for notes (merge the columns in these rows to make one row). Notes include information such as the title number, title, and source.

- Single space entries in columns.

- Use left alignment if all columns consist of words, figures, or years.

Year	Individual	Team
2006	202	11,334
2007	21,125	144,336
2008	2,156	14,441

- Use right alignment if columns need to be added, compared, or contrasted.

- If acceptable to the proper authority, use the *autofit* feature of the table function to adjust the width of the columns to fit the column text.

- Use singular forms for column headings (*Year* instead of *Years*).

- Use bold font for the column headings.

- Capitalize the first letter of each word in column headings (excluding *a, an, the, and, or, of, in,* etc.).

- Single space column headings into as many as five lines, and align at the bottom if line lengths are unequal.

- Use abbreviations (*Acct. No.* instead of *Account Number*) or smaller font to shorten column heading lengths.

- Center tables vertically and horizontally if they occupy the entire page.

Tables

Year	Individual	Team
2006	202	11,334
2007	21,125	144,336
2008	2,156	14,441

- Add a title number and title (if applicable) in uppercase letters to the top row and align to the left. Titles are numbered consecutively throughout the document (1, 2, 3, 4), within each chapter (1-1, 1-2, 1-3), or within each appendix (A-1, A-2, A-3).

- Add footnotes (if applicable) to the bottom row and align these to the left.

Table B-6 RACING POINTS		
Year	Individual	Team
2006	202	1,334
2007	21,125	144,336
2008	2,156	14,441
Source: *Racing Book of Facts*, 2009, p. 11.		

Notice the blank rows at the top and bottom of the table now contain notes.

- Other appearance improvements (i.e. shading, boldfacing font, centering the title, or indenting footnotes) can be added if acceptable to the proper authority. Leave one blank line above and below notes.

Table B-6 RACING POINTS		
Year	Individual	Team
2006	202	1,334
2007	21,125	144,336
2008	2,156	14,441
Source: *Racing Book of Facts*, 2009, p. 11.		

Tables Within Text

- Locate tables on the page where the reference to them begins.

- Avoid breaking a table at the bottom of the page. Instead, locate the table at the top of the next page and provide a cross reference to that page in parentheses.

(See Table 3.2 on page 41)

- Center tables horizontally within established margins, and indent at least .5 inch from each side margin. Table width must not exceed the width of the text.

- Leave one line between the text and the table on the top and bottom.

Tables:
Within Text

are achieved by establishing points for every race the driver or team enters. Points are based on a variety of factors, and three years have been calculated:

Table B-6 RACING POINTS		
Year	Individual	Team
2006	202	1,334
2007	21,125	144,336
2008	2,156	14,441
Source: *Racing Book of Facts*, 2009, p. 11.		

Drivers understand this system and work to attain the most points possible. Their racing careers often hinge on the scores they achieve as individual and on teams.

Tables Within Text

Tables on Separate Pages

Tables:
On Separate
Pages

- Tables that require a full page are centered vertically and horizontally within the established margins. If no margins have been established, leave a 1 inch minimum on all sides.

- If a document contains many tables that require a full page, the tables should be listed in an appendix. For convenience, all tables (including those that do not require a full page) can be listed in this appendix.

- If a table is located on another page or in an appendix, provide a cross reference to that page in parentheses.

Tables Containing Braced Column Headings

- Complex tables often have headings that straddle two or more columns.

- Center the braced column headings over the appropriate columns.

- Center the other column headings and text between the vertical rules.

Table 6 RETAIL AND WHOLESALE SALES 2006 to 2008				
Year	Retail		Wholesale	
	Sales $	% of Total Sales	Sales $	% of Total Sales
2006	$211,000	14.0	$1,300,000	86.0
2007	214,000	13.2	1,400,000	86.8
2008	204,000	10.2	1,800.000	89.8

Table Containing Braced Column Headings

Tables Containing Only Words

- Capitalize the first word of each item in text (excluding *a, an, the, and, or, of, in,* etc.).

- Leave one blank line above and below the text.

- Do not use a period after the entered items unless they comprise a complete sentence.

- Indent turnover lines *or* separate items with a blank line.

Paper, pens, pencils, rulers,
staplers, and notebooks

Computer, keyboard, mouse,
modem, router, speakers, and
hard drive

or

Paper, pens, pencils, rulers,
staplers, and notebooks

Computer, keyboard, mouse,
modem, router, speakers, and hard
drive

Table Containing Only Words

Tables Containing Only Figures

- Align whole numbers to the right.
- Align numbers with decimal points at the decimal point.
- Align hourly figures of time at the right.
- Align hour and minute figures at the colon.
- Align starting and ending times at the dash.

4173	25.29	11 a.m.	3:44 p.m.	7:32–8:44
24	12497.24	2 p.m.	12:00 noon	10:21–11:15
954	2.33	12 noon	2:23 a.m.	1:12–2:30
8	667.09	12 midnight	12:00 midnight	3:35–3:57

Tables Containing Money

- Insert a $ before the first amount at the head of the column and again at the total.

**Tables:
Containing
Money**

$ 27.00
142.50
1,206.54
$1,376.04

Tables Containing Percentages

- Insert a percent sign (%) unless the column heading designates such.

- Align at the decimal point and add zeros after the decimal point so all percentages align at the right.

**Tables:
Containing
Percentages**

- Add a zero to the left of the decimal point if numbers are less than 1 percent.

Increase

56.78%
1.49%
2.00%
0.67%

Table Leaders

- Use leaders to clarify if columns vary greatly in length.

**Tables:
Leaders**

- Use at least three periods per leader.

- Use *NA* if not available or not applicable.

TABLE 5	
IDAHO PLANT EXPENSES	
2009	
Division	**$**
Plant maintenance, grounds control, and field repair..................………	$440,000
Finance……………………........……...	310,000
Quality control…………………...........	350,000
Sales & marketing……........……….…	NA

Long Tables

- Try to avoid putting tables on more than one page. However, if this is absolutely necessary due to the length, then add a continuation note in parentheses under the table.

Bottom row is as follows:

(continued on page 21)

- At the top of the next page, add *continued* in parentheses next to the table number.

Top row of next page is as follows:

Table 6 (Continued)

Tables Converted to Graphs

- Tables can be converted to pie charts, line graphs, bar charts, etc. if this makes the data easier to understand.
- Always check with the proper authority to determine if converting tables to graphs is acceptable.

Index

APA: THE EASY WAY!

For many writers, the most difficult part of writing a research paper is the mechanics of putting that paper together... the detailed specifications regarding spacing, capitalization, citing of sources, etc. Many researchers deplore this part of the project and long to simply blurt out research findings...without any regard for spelling, punctuation, grammar, or protocol.

This book simplifies the mechanics of communicating an idea or ideas to others in a scholarly fashion. The writer must abide by the rules and regulations governing the publication of research...so writers need to learn what the rules are and conform to them accordingly. Consequently, ideas will be properly explained, communicated, understood, and appreciated.

MLA: THE EASY WAY!

This book clarifies important aspects of Modern Language Association (MLA) guidelines by providing excellent supplemental support. Frequently used aspects of MLA style, citation, and referencing are addressed in a simple format that allows researchers to focus on content instead of mechanics and style.

The intent of this handbook is simply to supplement the official *MLA Handbook for Writers of Research Papers* (6th edition). It is provided as a condensed version of the actual manual. It is not intended to supersede the manual, rather reduce its complexity.

Quite simply, *MLA: The Easy Way!* presents the basics of MLA style in a clear, concise, accurate, and easy-to-navigate package. Try it, and immediately relieve some of the stress of writing a research paper.

Chicago Manual of Style (CMS): The Easy Way!

This book covers many of the detailed specifications of the Chicago style…including spacing, margins, capitalization, citing of sources, etc. It also contains suggestions that enable the reader to fulfill CMS rules and regulations while focusing on the content, rather than the format, of the actual document. Adherence to the rules and regulation in this book will ensure that valuable and hard-earned research will be presented in the proper, professional, and scholarly manner it deserves.

Turabian: The Easy Way!

Years of experience have proven that there are consistent questions and misunderstandings regarding Turabian writing style. This book has been developed to simplify the Turabian writing experience. It is provided as a condensed version of the official *A Manual for Writers of Research Papers, Theses, and Dissertations* (7th edition). Students no longer have to navigate through the cumbersome and complicated official guide. This handbook is simple to use and far less time consuming. Thus, the title: *Turabian: The Easy Way!*

The book is divided into five parts. Part one focuses on the mechanics of Turabian style writing; part two emphasizes planning, drafting, and revising a research document; part three describes punctuation and writing style; part four explains source citations; and part five provides a sample paper.

Education is one of the best investments you will ever make…and our books maximize that investment!

Houghton & Houghton